A

LITURGICAL

GLOSSARY

compiled by

Michael Sansom

Canon-Residentiary, St. Albans Abbey; Director of Ordinands, diocese of St. Albans

GROVE BOOKS LIMITED
Bramcote   Nottingham   NG9 3DS

INTRODUCTION AND ACKNOWLEDGEMENTS
(FIRST EDITION)

Liturgy is a subject which very quickly throws up a barrage of unfamiliar words to defeat the student, the lay enquirer—and even a good many clergy.

The basis of this glossary was a simple word list compiled for students in the Cambridge Federation of Theological Colleges, but it has been expanded and rewritten by students at Ridley Hall. To those who have taken part in the labours—Mary Hayter, Tim Jenkins, Tim West, Nick Parish, Robert Ivell, Sam Randall, Chris Bracegirdle, Bill Atkins, John Holbrook, Matthew Strong, Gary Renison, Phil Clements, and Tony Gibson, together with June Smith who assisted with the typing, I give my grateful thanks.

Where a word included in the main glossary listing occurs within the definition of another word, then it is printed in **bold type** the first time it occurs in that entry. Definitions often refer to uses in Eastern Orthodoxy or in the Roman Catholic Church or elsewhere without prejudice to any value-judgments in respect of the items. In general the intention has been to restrict the contents to 'glossary' information, and to stop short of providing a liturgical dictionary.

Michael Sansom

NOTE RE SECOND EDITION

I am delighted that the first edition of the Glossary has sold out, and I have marginally revised the text, amending misprints and obscurities, for this second edition.

M.C.S. October, 1990

First Edition June 1985

Second Edition (by Grove Books Limited) November 1990

ISSN 0306-0609

ISBN 1 85174 158 5

THE GLOSSARY

ABLUTIONS. The ceremonial cleansing of the eucharistic vessels and of the minister's fingers after the eucharist.

ACCLAMATIONS. These are congregational interjections in the **eucharistic prayer** which may be described as 'a declaration of the congregation's faith in the meaning and purpose of the eucharistic celebration'. Eastern Orthodox worship has been familiar with acclamations for many centuries and these are the inspiration for those in modern eucharistic texts. They usually follow the **institution narrative.** The Church of England introduced them in Series 3.

AFFUSION. The pouring of water on the candidate at baptism. From an early time it was allowed as an alternative to immersion. The size of most fourth and fifth century baptistries would indicate that total immersion was not practised but that the baptizand stood knee-deep and had water poured over him. The difference between affusion and **aspersion** is only the amount of water involved. Cyprian says aspersion was usual in the case of **clinical baptism.** The BCP expresses a preference for immersion but allows pouring 'if they certify a child is weak'.

AGAPE (Greek, 'love'). A distinctively Christian word which, as a proper noun, denotes a 'love-feast' or fellowship-meal. In the early Church the Agape has at least semi-liturgical features, but its precise associations with the eucharist are disputed. Abuses brought the love-feast into disrepute by the eighth century and it had been largely suppressed. Its revivals hardly affected major denominations until J. Wesley, influenced by the Moravian Agape, introduced it to Methodism. In the twentieth century there have been further revivals, particularly in connection with ecumenism, with breakfasts following parish communion, and with the charismatic movement. Since Vatican II, limited use of the Agape has been encouraged in Roman Catholic Churches.

AGNUS DEI. Latin for the opening words of the anthem 'Lamb of God, you take away the sins of the world.' It is of Eastern origin and has been included in the Roman rite since the seventh century. It is used in liturgy to accompany the **fraction,** or as a communion anthem.

ALB. A long white tunic reaching to the feet. Originally of linen but now often of cotton or synthetic fibre, collarless and with close-fitting sleeves, it derives from the clerical tunic worn by professional people in the Graeco-Roman world. It became a specifically Christian vestment in the fifth century, being seen as a symbol of purity. A priest would say 'make me white' when putting it on. It was worn by all ranks of clergy until the eleventh century, when the **surplice** replaced it (especially in Northern Europe) for non-eucharistic worship. Today it is normally worn at eucharistic worship, usually underneath a **chasuble, dalmatic** or **tunicle.** Recent years have seen the creation of the cassock-alb, worn with or without a hood in place of **cassock** and surplice or alb and chasuble.

ALLELUIA. As a liturgical expression of praise, was taken over into the liturgy of the Church at an early date (lit. 'Praise Yah'). In the Roman rite it is sung at all Masses except in Lent, and occurs as the response to a verse from scripture after the second lesson (Epistle).

ALMUCE. Garment worn to protect the head and shoulders from cold weather. Originating in medieval times it consisted of either a lined hood or fur scarf worn over the surplice, evolving into a fur-lined hood with two ends hanging down in front. It became a mark of rank, the colour and type of fur having hierarchical significance. Usage was discontinued in the Established Church in Elizabethan times, generally being replaced by a black **tippet** or **scarf.**

ALTAR. Ancient title for the table where the eucharist is celebrated. This was changed to 'table' or 'holy table' by the English and other reformers.

AMBO (Greek 'reading desk', 'ridge' of a hill). A form of lectern or reading desk of pulpit proportions but not originally designed to be the place from which the sermon was to be delivered, constructed from a variety of materials and often decorated, especially in larger **basilicas.** Functioning as the place used for the gospel reading it was large enough to accommodate both reader and candle bearers. Smaller designs are known and were utilized for the other eucharistic lessons. The practice of preaching from the ambo (instead of from the bishop's seat) is thought to have been introduced by John Chrysostom c.400 as he had a weak voice.

AMICE. Rectangular piece of linen, with strings attached. White, originally a neckerchief, it is worn round the neck and was designed to protect other vestments from sweat. Originating in the sixth century, it became an essential mass vestment in the West by the eighth century.

ANAMNESIS. Greek for memorial, remembrance or recalling. The word is used in the narrative of the Lord's Supper in 1 Cor. 11. 24f and Luke 22.19. In liturgical study it refers to that part of the **eucharistic prayer** in which we speak of the reason for our celebration and in most liturgies it follows the words of the **institution narrative.** The formal norm of the anamnesis comprises a statement of what is remembered and a statement of what is done in remembrance of Christ. Important doctrinal question are involved and the wording of the anamnesis in modern eucharistic texts is a major area of controversy.

ANAPHORA (Greek 'offering'). The central prayer in the eucharistic liturgy, this has commonly been called the prayer of **consecration** in English rites but the **canon** in the Roman rite. An anaphora will contain most if not all of the following components: (1)**sursum corda,** (2) **preface,** (3) **sanctus,** (4) **benedictus qui venit,** (5) **institution narrative,** (6) **anamnesis,** (7) **epiclesis,** and (8) **doxology.** The anaphora is also known as the **great thanksgiving** or **eucharistic prayer.**

ANTEPENDIUM. A veil in front of the **altar.** It may have been used as a protection from dust when altars were constructed with a latticed front.

ANTHEM. The Anglicized form of the word **antiphon.** Traditionally it refers to a musical setting of words drawn from the psalms or scripture. In the Anglican service the proper place for the anthem is after the third collect at Morning and Evening prayer, as prescribed by the 1662 rubric at this point: 'In quires and places where they sing, here followeth the anthem.'

ANTIDORON. Remains of the loaves from which the bread for the Eastern Orthodox Eucharist is cut and which is distributed at the end of the liturgy. The practice developed at a time when non-communicating attendance was increasing. The laity only received tokens of the holy thing (Greek 'instead of the gift') and not the reality. Its use is regarded as sharing in some measure in the eucharistic blessing and hence non-orthodox visitors are encouraged to receive.

ANTIPHON derives from the Greek **antiphonon** ('something sung alternately by two choirs'). In the Western Church the word denotes sentences, usually scriptural, recited before and after both the psalms and **canticles** in the divine **office.** They vary with the feast and season. In the Eastern Church the word has a different meaning, being applied to the three anthems sung antiphonally in the early part of the eucharistic liturgy and varying according to the feast or season.

APSE. A vaulted, semi-circular or polygonal end of the **chancel.** It was the standard form of the **sanctuary** in early Christian **basilicas**, usually projecting beyond the east end.

ASHLAR. Masonry comprising largish blocks wrought to have even faces and dressed—as opposed to randomly constructed stonework.

ASPERGES. The sprinkling of holy water (usually with a sprinkler consisting of a perforated ball with a handle or a brush known as an aspergillium). In Roman Catholic circles the people would formerly have been asperged before each sung eucharist. Nowadays it occurs specifically at the Easter Vigil after the blessing of the water and at the feast of the Baptism of Jesus as a reminder to the congregations of their own baptism. It may be used on other occasions as may seem appropriate. In monastic communities it is used after **compline** each evening. Asperges may be used at the dedication of a building or blessing of crops. It is first attested in the eighth century.

ASPERSION. Alternative title for **sprinkling** in baptism. See **affusion.**

AUMBRY. A recess or cupboard in the wall of a church or sacristy designed to hold vessels for mass and communion. The reserved sacrament may be kept in an aumbry in Anglican churches but this is forbidden by the Roman Church.

BALDACHINO see **ciborium** (2).

BALDAQUIN see **ciborium** (2).

BASILICA. An aisled hall, usually with an apsidal end, together with a large rectangular central area lined on each side with columns and side aisles. As an architectural form, it was not religious in origin, being originally utilized as a place for the administration of justice. The placing of an **altar** in an **apse** at the east end created a centre of focus for Christian worship.

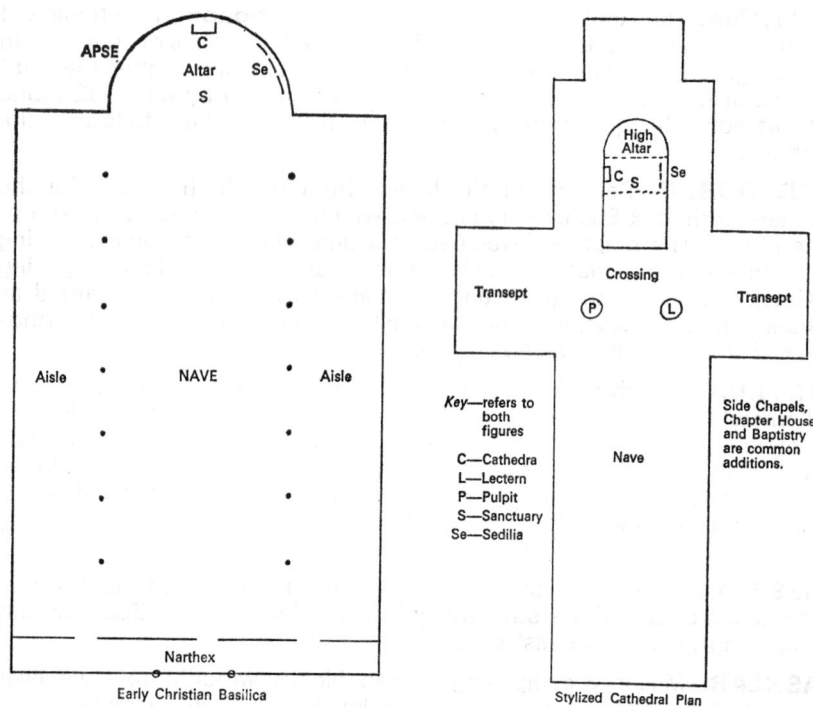

APSE

C
Altar   Se
S

High
Altar
C S   Se

Crossing

Transept   (P)   (L)   Transept

Aisle   NAVE   Aisle

Key—refers to
both
figures

C—Cathedra
L—Lectern
P—Pulpit
S—Sanctuary
Se—Sedilia

Nave

Side Chapels,
Chapter House
and Baptistry
are common
additions.

Narthex

Early Christian Basilica

Stylized Cathedral Plan

BEMA. A space raised above the level of the **nave** of a church, which is shut off by the **iconostasis** and contains the **altar** (i.e. the counterpart of the **sanctuary** in the west). Originally a platform in ancient Athenian places of public assembly (cf. Acts. 18.12, Rom. 14.10).

BENEDICTION. (1) the authoritative pronouncement of God's favour. In liturgy, this takes the form of blessing of **elements** in **consecration.** Also, blessings are pronounced at the end of a service and are given to individuals such as to the deacon who is to read the gospel, the penitent about to make a confession, and to the unconfirmed at a communion service. Pronouncements of a benediction have become the common practice to conclude liturgical services. (2) from the eleventh century, there has been the practice of exposing the sacrament for veneration. This action is completed by the blessing of the congregation with the sacred **host.** From the sixteenth century, it has been the practice for the host to be exposed in a **monstrance** placed on or above the **altar.** A short service is concluded by the blessing of the congregation with the host. Because mass could not, until the 1950s, be celebrated later than noon, this rite was favoured for evening devotions, but evening masses have now often replaced it. In the Church of England there is no rubrical or other encouragement to follow this counter-reformation use.

BENEDICTUS QUI VENIT. An **anthem** usually said or sung after the **sanctus.** It was retained in the 1549 BCP but was dropped in 1552. It has more recently been restored in many Anglican rites. The title comes from the opening words in Latin 'Blessed is he who comes . . .' (cf. Matt. 21.9).

BIDDING OF THE BEDES. An early English term for the 'saying of prayers' in the vernacular before, after or in place of the sermon. To 'bid a bead' means to 'offer a prayer', (German, *beten,* 'pray'). These prayers 'for all conditions of men' came to be known in French as *'Formules du Prone'* and in English as 'Bidding Prayers'. See **prone, suffrages.**

BLACK LETTER DAYS. The lesser (mainly non-scriptural) Saints' Days (printed in black in the calendar) and feast days, opposed to the major festivals which formerly appeared in red letters in the (BCP) calendar. The practice of distinguishing important feasts by the use of red letters goes back to the pre-Reformation service books. Today, if they are not distinguished in the lectionary by colour, they may be distinguished by using a heavier type-face for Red Letter days, but the ASB does not have precisely the same distinctions.

BLACK RUBRIC. A rubric concerning kneeling at communion, added by Order in Council to the 1552 BCP, omitted in 1559, and restored (with a tiny change) by Parliament in 1662. It was originally called the 'Declaration on Kneeling' and the title 'Black Rubric' seems to date from the nineteenth century.

BREVIARY. The result of abbreviating and combining several books into one, it is a liturgical book containing the psalms, hymns, lessons, and antiphons, recited at the daily **office.** The Roman breviary has now been revised and called 'The Liturgy of the Hours' 1971 for daily use by both clergy and the people. Morning and Evening Prayer in the BCP were derived from the pre-reformation Breviary.

BURSE. A case consisting of two squares of stiffened material (usually varying in colour according to season) in which the **corporal, pall,** and **purificators** may be kept. Often placed on top of the vessels except during the **anaphora.**

CANCELLI. Ballustrading used for the demarcation of the **sanctuary.**

CANDLES. See **lights.**

CANON (Greek, *kanon,* 'rule'). The fixed unchanging part of the **eucharistic prayer.** The term was in the Middle Ages applied in Western rites to the parts following the **sanctus,** and this was virtually identical throughout the West, but it more recently may have been used to mean the whole **eucharistic prayer** (or **anaphora**). The canon was truncated to the **institution narrative** in most Reformed rites, but was retained in its former shape by Cranmer in the 1549 BCP. It was then split in the 1552 BCP into the Prayer for the Church Militant, a shortened prayer including the **institution narrative** and the **prayer of oblation.** The Tridentine Mass with the Roman canon at its heart remained virtually unchanged from 1570 until after the Second Vatican Council.

CANTICLE (Latin, *canticulum,* 'a little song'). It refers to a song or prayer (other than one of the psalms) derived usually from the Bible, which is used in the liturgical worship of the Church. The Latin names of canticles (e.g. Magnificat and Nunc Dimittis) derive from the opening words of the Latin versions.

CAPITULUM. Refers either to (1) 'The Little Chapter' said at most of the canonical hours, after the psalms, consisting of scriptural verses or to (2) an **anthem** in the Ambrosian Rite said at **lauds** after the psalm and before the **antiphon.**

CASSOCK. Ankle-length tunic with narrow sleeves. Originally a general garment but when, under Barbarian influence in the sixth century, shorter garments were adopted, the clergy retained the longer cassock, for outdoor dress, rather than for worship. In 1604, Canon Law expected that Anglican clergy would wear a garment of this sort continually in public. This practice largely ceased in the nineteenth century. It is not a vestment, although universally worn under them, nor an exclusively clerical garb, being worn by servers, choristers and others.

CATHEDRA. The bishop's chair or throne in his cathedral church. The original position was in the centre of the **apse** behind the high **altar.** In the Middle Ages it was placed in the **chancel.**

CHANCEL (Latin, *cancellus,* 'ballustrade'). Originally it referred to the part of the church reserved for officiating clergy, divided from the rest of the church by low screens. When the area containing the **altar** was separated off as the **sanctuary,** 'chancel' was used to refer to the section between the sanctuary and **nave.** It is sometimes known as the choir (or **'quire').** The north side is known as *'cantoris'* (the cantor's), the south as *'decani'* (the dean's).

CHANTRY. A chapel attached to, or inside a church, originally endowed for the saying of masses for the soul of the founder or for some other individual.

CHASUBLE. Outermost eucharistic vestment, worn over the **alb,** usually only worn by the president. Derived from **'paenula'** or **'planeta',** the outer cloak worn by all in the Graeco-Roman world. Originally tent-shaped, with a hole for the head, it gradually reduced in size. Retained in the 1549 prayer book, but abolished in the 1552 prayer book, the chasuble fell out of use in the Church of England until the ceremonial revival of the nineteenth century.

CHERUBIKON. The 'Cherubic Hymn' sung by the choir in Eastern Orthodox rites at the great **entrance.** Three forms are used, one ordinary form, one for the **presanctified** elements and one for Maundy Thursday and Easter Eve. The hymns were composed in the late sixth century.

CHIMERE. Silk or satin sleeveless gown, black or scarlet, worn by Anglican bishops and doctors of divinity. Originally a short cloak worn by bishops when riding horseback, it became, in longer form, part of the customary attire of bishops at both liturgical and civil functions.

CHRISM. A mixture of olive oil and perfume, usually balsam, consecrated in the Roman rite by the bishop after the first ablution of the mass on Maundy Thursday. It is used to anoint candidates for baptism, confirmation, and ordination, and also in the blessing of the baptismal **font** and the consecration of **chasubles, altars,** chalices, **patens,** and bells. Chrism oil is also used in some Anglican circles.

CHRISMATION. Anointing with **chrism.**

CHRYSOM *or* **CHRISOM.** The baptism gown of infants. In the early church, baptizands were given a white robe on leaving the **font,** and wore it on all liturgical occasions in Easter week. John the deacon says it represents 'the raiment of glory' so that, clad in a wedding garment, he may approach the table of the heavenly bridegroom as a new man. A white head-dress was also worn which, for John the deacon, represents priesthood. In the west, by the middle ages, the white head-dress was all that was left, given with the words 'receive this white garment and bear it stainless before the judgment seat of Christ'. It had been reduced to white bands tied on the forehead and had the practical function of protecting the **chrism,** with which the neophye had been anointed, from defilement. Here it became known as the chrismale or chrysom-cloth.

CIBORIUM. (1) A cup, usually with a lid, in which the bread is placed. It may be used in place of a **paten.** Sometimes the lid is itself a paten. (2) A canopy of wood, stone or metal over an altar. Now more usually called a **baldachino,** but baldachino is also used of a portable canopy of fabric carried in processions.

CINCTURE. A band of material, usually worn around the waist of a cassock in place of a belt or girdle.

CLERESTORY (pron. 'clear-storey'). The upper storey of the nave walls of large churches built to provide additional lighting through the pierced windows.

CLINICAL BAPTISM (Greek *kline,* 'bed'). Death-bed or emergency baptism. In the early church, magistrates or soldiers whose livelihood might involve taking life, or others whose livelihood compromised Christian values, postponed baptism until the end of their lives. Constantine was baptized on his death-bed. Now usually restricted to infants in danger of death.

COLOURS, LITURGICAL. To mark seasons in the ecclesiastical calendar many churches follow a colour-sequence for vestments and other liturgical objects. The use of a colour-sequence—differing from later practice notably by advocating black for Christmas—is first attested in twelfth century Jerusalem. Innocent III (1198-1216) outlined the now-familiar pattern: white—feasts; red—martyrs; black/purple—penitential seasons; green—**feria** and non-festival Sundays. The associations are largely psychological; it seems 'natural' to use fiery blood-red for martyrs and Pentecost. The Roman Church did not define its rule before 1570. The post-Vatican II **missal** recognizes five colours (white, red, violet, rose, green). Eastern Orthodoxy has no strict colour rules. In Britain, Calvinist and Puritan influenced churches reject colour-sequences. The Anglo-Catholic Movement prompted many Anglicans to reintroduce them and they occur in the ASB.

COLLECT FOR PURITY. Cranmer's (free) translation of an older Latin prayer used in the preparation of the priest in the Sarum Missal. 'Almighty God to whom all hearts are open . . .'.

COLLECT. A brief prayer consisting of an opening address, petition and closing doxology. It is uncertain whether the name is intended to suggest (a) that the prayer sums up (collects) the theme of the occasion or (b) that it is a prayer said when the congregation is assembled (collected). A collect is 'of' a day and 'for' the object of petition.

COMFORTABLE WORDS. The name given to four verses of scripture (Matt. 11.28, John 3.16, 1 Tim. 1.15, I John 2.1) in the eucharist. They follow the confession and absolution in the BCP and precede them in the ASB. They form the scriptural warrant for the words of the absolution.

COMMINATION (Latin *comminatio*—'curse'). Originally Ash Wednesday service of penitence and forgiveness, with solemn absolution marked by ashes applied to forehead. Radically altered by Cranmer in 1549 BCP and revised in 1552 and 1662, it became a complete service entitled 'A Commination against sinners or denouncing of God's anger and judgments' to be used on first day of Lent or at other times. The service consists of an exhortation, Psalm 51, **suffrages**, prayers and blessing.

COMMUNION IN ONE KIND. Partaking of both the bread and wine at the eucharist was general in the West until the twelfth century. By the thirteenth century receiving the bread alone was almost universal for the laity in the West. This was probably done to avoid the risk of spilling in an age when great importance was coming to be attached to the presence of the Person of Christ under the forms of bread and wine. Also in the thirteenth century the doctrine of concomitance—that either part of the the sacrament by itself mediates the whole Christ—became part of the dogmatic teaching of the Western church. The reformers insisted that only communication in both kinds had scriptural warrant. In the Roman church communion in one kind continues, although since Vatican II there is a move to 'restore the cup to the laity'.

COMMUNICANTES (Latin, 'communicating'). The opening word of the third paragraph of the Tridentine Roman **canon,** developing the preceding **memento** by referring to the communion of saints. Besides Mary and Joseph (in more modern rites), the names form two groups of twelve: eleven Apostles and Paul, and twelve martyrs (all Roman except for Cyprian) arranged in hierarchical order. Before 1570 local saints were sometimes added. Since 1969 nine of the apostles and all the martyrs may be omitted. Like **hanc igitur** and **qui pridie,** *Communicantes* is modified according to the ecclesiastical calendar for Christmas, Epiphany,(Maundy Thursday), Easter, Ascension, and Pentecost.

COMMIXTURE. This is the placing of a particle of the consecrated **host** in the chalice after the **fraction** at the eucharist. It appears to have derived from the **fermentum** and by the ninth century had become a way of consecrating extra chalices.

COMPETENTES. Those catechumens who had given their names at the beginning of Lent to be baptized at Easter. During Lent they would undergo a course of daily instruction and daily **exorcism** (see also **disciplina arcani, redditio symboli, scrutiny**).

COMPLINE. Established by Benedict as a retiring office for religious communities. Parts of Compline are used in Evening Prayer of the BCP, including the **nunc dimittis** and the collect, 'Lighten our darkness . . .'. Details of the service vary, but normally it consists of an evening hymn, psalms, and prayers.

CONCELEBRATION. In the West, the recital of the **eucharistic prayer** (or parts of it) by two or more priests together, with or without comparable ceremonial.

CONFITEOR (Latin 'I confess'). Any confession of sin.

CONSECRATION, PRAYER OF. The title first given in the 1662 Book of Common Prayer, to that section of the **eucharistic prayer** which contains the **institution narrative.** It begins 'Almighty God, our heavenly Father, who of thy tender mercy . . .'. It is sometimes used to refer to the whole eucharistic prayer, sometimes to that part that follows **sanctus.** Because it is both confusing and controversial, its use ought to be avoided except with reference to the BCP.

CONSIGNATION. (1) The signing of the cross with **chrism** at confirmation. In the West it became a synonym for confirmation. (2) The signing of the chalice with the broken **host** in Eastern Orthodox rites.

CONSIGNATORIUM. A name used after the ninth century for the chrismation or room where **consignation** took place at baptism.

COPE. Ceremonial version of an outdoor garment worn in Roman times. A semi-circular piece of cloth, worn around the shoulders and held together by a clasp at the front. Generally worn at non-eucharistic services, when the **chasuble** is not used. Not a specifically clerical vestment, the cope is a general ecclesiastical robe for ceremonial occasions. Originally it had a hood, which survives today as a triangular ornament on the back of the garment.

CORPORAL. Piece of white linen, some 20 inches square, on which the chalice and **paten** are placed during the eucharistic consecration.

COTTA. Short-sleeved, waist-length version of the **surplice** with a square-cut yoke at the neck.

CREDENCE TABLE. A shelf or side-table for sacramental vessels— usually placed in the **sanctuary.**

CROSSING. The space, usually under the central tower, at the intersection of the **nave, chancel** and **transepts.**

CRUET. Flask, now usually of glass, containing wine or water. Sometimes replaced by silver or pewter flagon. Kept on **credence.**

CUSHAPA. Private prayer recited quietly by the priest kneeling in the Nestorian rite.

DALMATIC. A tunic usually worn over an **alb** by the deacon. It derives from a popular garment worn in second century Rome. Originally white and made of linen or wool, it came later to be coloured and made of silk or other materials. In mediaeval times it seems to have been identical with the **tunicle**, from which it is likely nowadays to be distinguished by two coloured strips running over the shoulders (as opposed to one). Also worn by the sovereign at Coronation.

DEPRECATIO. An act of intercessory prayer, a litany for the church universal, it is mainly of Eastern origin. The earliest known version, that ascribed to Pope Gelasius (492-496 AD), 'Deprecatio Gelasii', comes from a collection of private prayers from France of the ninth century.

DIALOGUE. The opening section of the **eucharistic prayer** in which there is a dialogue between president and people. It contains (a) a mutual greeting, (b) the **sursum corda,** and (c) gratias agamus.

DIRECTORY. A book containing directions concerning the shape and content of public worship but not liturgical texts.

DIRGE. The name given to the service of **mattins** and **lauds** from mediaeval times said for the dead before burial. The name derives from the **antiphon** 'Dirige Domine Deus . . .' from Ps. 5.8 (see **placebo**).

DISCIPLINA ARCANI. The discipline of secrecy practised by the church in the fourth, fifth, and sixth centuries, possibly as a result of persecution, or as a device to prevent blasphemy and profanation, the secraments were only celebrated in conditions of utmost secrecy. Possibly the church was influenced by the mystery cults. After the Bible readings and sermon, the **missa catechumenorum,** the catechumens were dismissed from the service and the doors locked. Only the baptized were permitted to take part in the intercessions and the eucharist itself, the **missa fidelium.** The creeds and Lord's Prayer were left secret and only revealed to the **competentes** during their course of instruction (see **redditio symboli**).

DIPTYCHS. Lists of names of both the living and the departed for whom prayer is made in the Eastern Orthodox eucharist. The name is derived from a hinged board on which the names were once written. Strictly speaking it is inaccurate to talk of diptychs in the Western rites, where the practice was to recite the names of those offering the bread for the eucharist. In early times the diptychs were recited publicly and inclusion or exclusion of a name was regarded as a sign of communion or excommunication.

DOXOLOGY. A closing ascription of praise, concluding a prayer, psalm or canticle.

EASTER ANTHEMS. Derived from the mediaeval procession to the Easter sepulchre, they were the scriptural verses said at this point and formed an introduction to **mattins** of Easter Day in 1549 BCP. The Easter Anthems, including a new first anthem, replaced the Venite in the 1662 BCP at Morning Prayer on Easter Day.

ECTENIE (Greek 'instant', 'fervent'). Litany following the sermon in the Byzantine rite.

EFFETA. From 'ephthatha'—'be opened'—Mark 7.34: an anointing of the senses with oil or spittle. Originally the purpose was not to open but to close the senses after the **exorcism** which followed **scrutiny.** John the Deacon says: 'the ears were fortified so that they might permit entrance to nothing harmful which might entice them back' and the nose anointed to 'give no admittance to the pleasures of this world nor anything which might weaken their minds'. Ambrose of Milan however uses the formula

'Effeta, that is, be opened'. He does not say whether oil or spittle is used, and tries to explain the fact that the nostrils are anointed, instead of the mouth as in the Gospel story, by saying that it would be improper for a priest to touch the mouth of a woman. Later the rite was adapted to the Gospel story. In the Roman rite, spittle was used and in Spain and North Italy the mouth was touched rather than the nostrils.

EMBER DAYS. The etymology is uncertain, possibly from *quattuor tempora* (Latin, 'four seasons'). Originally associated with agriculture they came to be the occasion for ordinations, possibly as early as the third century, marked by prayer and fasting. In the Church of England they are observed as the Wednesday, Friday, and Saturday before ordinations in Lent, at Petertide, Michaelmas and Advent.

EMBOLISM. An expansion of the final two clauses of the Lord's Prayer said by the priest in all Eastern Orthodox liturgies except the Byzantine and the Abyssinian where a **doxology** alone is used as a conclusion. In the Roman mass it refers to the similar prayer which begins 'Deliver us, Lord, from every evil'.

ENARXIS (Greek 'opening', 'beginning'). The preparatory office in the Byzantine rite. Possibly in origin a processional rite, it takes place between the **prothesis** and little **entrance.** Introduced during the seventh or eighth century it consists of a blessing of the Trinity, three litanies, and three anthems.

ENTHRONEMENT. See Inthronization.

ENTRANCE, GREAT. The solemn 'offertory' procession in the Eastern Orthodox rites when the elements are carried from the **altar** of the **prothesis** to the main altar.

ENTRANCE, LITTLE. The liturgical procession of the gospel book in the Eastern Orthodox eucharist. The book is carried from the **sanctuary** through a side door in the **iconostasis** into the church and back through the central doors. This is accompanied by the singing of an entrance chant, a hymn and the **trisagion.**

EPICLESIS (Greek, 'invocation'). The petition during the **eucharistic prayer** for the work of the Holy Spirit. In some rites there is a 'double epiclesis', (i.e. an invocation of the Spirit before the **institution narrative** upon the bread and wine and after the **anamnesis** upon the people present). The history and theological significance of the epiclesis is highly controversial. In Eastern practice the epiclesis normally follows the institution narrative and anamnesis.

EUCHARISTIC PRAYER. Traditionally beginning at the **dialogue,** the amount of material it contains varies between different rites. For the various components that it may contain, see **anaphora.**

EUCHOLOGION. The Greek Orthodox book of prayers containing parts of the sacraments, services, occasional offices and blessings said by officiating ministers, i.e. bishop, priest and deacon. Often produced in two volumes, the Greater Euchologion contains **vespers, mattins,** the three eucharistic liturgies of St. Chrysostom, St. Basil and the **presanctified** and the six remaining sacraments. The smaller or Lesser Euchologion, also called 'the Book of Blessings', omits **vespers, mattins,** eucharistic liturgies, ordination and consecration of a church and includes the five remaining sacraments, funeral offices, occasional offices and blessings as commonly required.

EXOMOLOGESIS. The confession of sin in the early church. The word was applied to the whole process of confession, satisfaction and forgiveness by which the penitent sinner was reconciled to the church.

EXORCISM. A formal act or ceremony to drive the devil or unclean spirits away. In the early church, it formed an essential part of the rites of the catechumenate and baptism. Catechumens received exorcisms and salt as a protection against the devil. **Competentes** were regularly exorcized at each of the **scrutinies.** The modern Roman Catholic rite has retained exorcism as part of the baptism service. In the Church of England there has been no rite of exorcism since 1552.

EXTREME UNCTION. The last anointing, regarded as a sacrament by the Roman Catholic church. Those in danger of death are anointed with olive oil, which has been blessed by the bishop before the *pater noster* of the mass on Holy Thursday. It is believed to strengthen the soul, take away venial sin and temporal punishment, and may give health to the body. Traditionally only those who have been baptized and are in danger of death have been eligible to receive it. The priest makes the sign of the cross with his thumb after dipping it in oil, on the eyes, ears, nose, mouth, hands, and sometimes the feet, of the person in danger of death. He says 'through this most holy anointing and His tender mercy, may the Lord forgive you whatever sins you have committed by the sense of sight, smell, taste, and speech, and touch. Amen.' Since Vatican II the use of the sacrament has been extended to those not in danger of death, and the principal emphasis has been on the anointing of the sick with a view to healing.

EXULTET. See **lucernarium.**

FAIR WHITE LINEN CLOTH. A white linen runner on the communion table during the eucharist (as required by BCP opening rubric), but not to be confused with 'fair linen cloth' (the **corporal),** required by BCP rubric after communion.

FALDSTOOL. A folding stool (without a back) used in the **sanctuary** by a bishop when not occupying his throne. Sometimes, in Church of England, used of a litany-desk (although in style more akin to a **prie-dieu**).

FERIA. In classical Latin feria means 'feast day' or 'holiday' but in Roman ecclesiastical usage it is applied to those days (other than Saturdays or Sundays) on which no feast falls.

FERMENTUM. A fragment of the bread consecrated at an episcopal celebration of the eucharist and taken to a church where a presbyter was presiding. It was added to the chalice after the **fraction** as a symbol of unity. The custom had died out in the East by the fourth century but continued in Rome until the eighth or ninth century.

FONT. A ceremonial basin used for baptism, traditionally positioned near the entrance of a church building. Early fonts were quadrilateral in shape and were later succeeded by octagonal, circular, and cruciform configurations. Most of the various shapes are thought to reinforce the connexion between baptism and the death and resurrection of Christ.

FRACTION. The breaking of the bread for distribution. In the 1662 Book of Common Prayer it takes place during the **prayer of consecration.**

FRONTAL. Panel of cloth, often embroidered, hung in front of the **altar** (usually varying in colour according to season).

GLORIA IN EXCELSIS. Latin form of the opening words of 'Glory to God in the highest'. It is a hymn dating from the fourth century and was used at other services besides the eucharist. The opening sentence comes from the angels' song in Lk. 2.14.

GLORIA PATRI. (Latin, 'Glory to the Father'). The beginning of an ascription of glory to the three Persons of the Trinity. Also known as the 'lesser doxology' (the 'greater doxology' is **gloria in excelsis**), it is appended to canticles and psalms in many liturgies. Since the Arians used **doxologies** capable of unorthodox interpretation the form of the Gloria Patri became a test of orthodoxy.

GRADUAL. From Latin *gradus* ('step') it refers, in the Western church, to the set of **antiphons,** usually from the Psalms, sung between the epistle and the gospel. The name derives from the practice of singing it either on the **altar** steps or while the deacon was ascending the steps of the **ambo.** Originally it was only chanted by the cantors or choir; only from the later Middle Ages did the practice of recitation by the priest become established.

GREAT ENTRANCE. See **entrance, great.**

GREAT THANKSGIVING. A title sometimes used for **anaphora** or **eucharistic prayer.**

GREMIAL. A cloth used by a bishop (and sometimes others) to prevent his hands from soiling his vestments. It is spread on his lap when he sits for the **kyrie eleison, gloria in excelsis,** and creed. The use of gremials first appeared in Western liturgies at the end of the thirteenth century.

HANC IGITUR (Latin, 'this therefore'). The opening words of the fourth paragraph of the Tridentine **canon,** following **communicantes,** it is a prayer for the acceptance of the **oblation**; originally independent, perhaps part of the **litany** of intercession. Before the Gregorian reforms (590-604), the Hanc Igitur was variable with many additional clauses, used to express the particular intention of the mass. Some special formulae were allowed to remain, for example at Easter, Pentecost, and at a bishop's consecration.

HOST (Latin, *hostia*, 'victim', 'sacrifice'). A term from the Roman rite referring to the consecrated bread in the eucharist.

HOUR SERVICES. The services of the Daily **office.**

HOUSELLING cloth is a long white linen cloth spread before, or held by, the communicants when receiving the elements. 'Housel' is a mediaeval English name for the eucharist, hence 'to be houselled' is to receive communion.

HUMBLE ACCESS. The title of a prayer ('We do not presume . . .') in the 1548 Order of the Communion, and positioned before the people's communion. The name comes from the 1637 Scottish liturgy which called it a 'Collect of Humble Access'. From 1552 onwards it was placed after the **sanctus,** but recent Anglican rites place it before the Peace, or near to the reception of communion.

HUMERAL VEIL (humeral—of or relating to the humerus). Silk shawl laid round shoulders and serving to cover hands when carrying **paten** (in processions, **benediction,** etc.).

ICONOSTASIS. A screen found in Eastern Orthodox churches separating the **sanctuary** from the rest of the church. Early forms had small icons hanging but greater subsequent elaborations and permanence, rather than decoration at particular festivals, has caused the screens to hide the **altar** completely. Often a curtain known as a veil hangs behind the doors of the iconostasis.

INDENTED RUBRICS. Rubrics which are placed alongside the text to which they relate, and are 'indented' into the text—such as is often the case with **manual acts.**

INSTITUTION NARRATIVE. The account of the Last Supper which has as its core the words used by our Lord in instituting the eucharist, 'This is my Body', 'This is my Blood'. In the West from the early Middle Ages the narrative was regarded as consecrating the elements (see also **prayer of consecration,** and **supplementary consecration**).

INSUFFLATION. The blowing into the face of a baptizand with the command to receive the Holy Spirit as in John 20.22. It may be performed in modern Roman Catholic rites for admission to the catechumenate in the mission field where 'false worship flourishes'.

INTHRONIZATION. More usually referred to as enthronement. The ceremony in which the newly consecrated or translated diocesan bishop is installed in his cathedral. See **cathedra.**

INTINCTION. The practice of dipping the consecrated bread, or **host,** into consecrated or unconsecrated wine, in order to make communion easier for the sick, and for those who do not wish to drink directly from a common cup.

INTROIT. The chant which, in the Western church, forms the opening act of worship in the Mass. Originally it consisted of the whole psalm, sung with **antiphon** and **gloria patri,** and was sung as the president entered the church. It is thought to be of later origin than the **gradual,** from which it differs in not being an integral part of the service; it accompanies the entrance procession.

INVITATORY. Found in the Latin **breviary,** it is Psalm 95, **venite,** with its corresponding **antiphon,** which begins the first daily **office.** Until recently it came at the beginning of **mattins,** but the 1971 Roman breviary ordered that it be said before either **lauds** or the Office of Readings if they preceded Mattins. Psalms 23, 66, and 99 (Vulg.) were provided as alternatives. In the BCP Venite is retained at Morning Prayer, but the antiphon is discarded.

KYRIE ELEISON (Greek, 'Lord have mercy'). The first evidence of its use as a response to the petitions of a **litany** comes from fourth century Jerusalem and Antioch. At Rome, an intercessory litany of this type **(deprecatio** gelasii) was included from the fifth century to follow the **introit** of the mass. The litany had disappeared completely by the end of the eighth century and the acclamations were arranged as a nine-fold kyrie (Kyrie eleison three times, Christe eleison three times, Kyrie eleison three times).

LAUDS. One of the oldest parts of the divine **office,** it is the traditional morning prayer of the Western Church. It includes Pss. 148-150 where the word *'laudate'* occurs (Latin, 'praise'). In the BCP parts of lauds and **mattins** were combined to form Morning Prayer.

LAVABO. Taken from Ps. 26.6—'I will wash my hands in innocency'— this verse is recited at the ceremonial washing of the president's hands at the eucharist. Since the middle ages, the washing has occured after the reception of gifts, symbolizing cleansing.

LECTIO CONTINUA. The prescribed continuous reading of Scripture on either a day-to-day or a Sunday-to-Sunday basis.

LECTIO ELECTA. The system of daily reading of Scripture whereby the readings are chosen each day and not on a continuous basis.

LECTIONARY. The book containing the extracts ('pericopes') from Scripture appointed to be read in public worship. 'Lectionary' may be used in a narrower sense to designate a manuscript (especially in Greek) with the pericopes written out in full, or in a general sense to describe any scheme of reading of scripture on a calendrical basis.

LIGHTS. Their liturgical use is based on inextricable combinations of utilitarian, devotional, symbolic, and ceremonial origins. Principally: (a) candles placed on and/or around the **altar** (the latter practice being of greater antiquity and emphasizing their processional nature) and lit during liturgical observances; (b) a large single candle, on the north side of the sanctuary, in use during Eastertide, and thereafter placed near the font for use at baptisms (paschal candle) (c) a light burning continuously before an **aumbry** or **tabernacle** containing the Reserved Sacrament (sanctuary lamp) (d) a lighted candle given, after baptism, to a candidate, parent, or godparent, indicating progress from darkness to light, etc.

LITANY (Greek, 'supplication'). A responsive form of prayer. The lesser litany of the Eastern Church forms an introduction to formal prayers. It is brief and of general content. The lesser litany of BCP **mattins** is the responsive 'Lord have mercy . . .'. The greater litany of the Eastern Church contains a number of intercessory biddings.

17

LITURGICAL MOVEMENT. The title of a movement for liturgical renewal of the twentieth century, though its origins are earlier. The major concerns have been for full participation by the worshippers in the action of the liturgy, including emphasis upon the authenticity and intelligibility of liturgical celebration and of its language and presentation.

LITURGY. Used by Eastern Orthodox to refer to the eucharist but in the West more generally to refer to any written text for use in Christian worship.

LOW MASS. In the Western church it is usually understood as a simplified form of the mass. Its roots are in the middle ages when it was impractical to carry out all the usual ceremonial when a priest said mass daily. The service is normally said rather than sung, often without assisting ministers except a single server. It is the usual form of celebration except on Sundays and greater feast days, when at least one service is a high mass.

LUCERNARIUM. The blessing of the evening lamp with a thanksgiving to God for the day, a Jewish practice surviving within early Christianity. Originally part of the monastic night office, it survives principally in the lighting of the Paschal Candle from the New Fire during the Easter Eve Vigil, accompanied by the singing of a chant or blessing, the **exultet**— a seventh century composition with the theme of Christ's triumph over darkness.

MANIPLE. A strip of material, usually sik, looped over left wrist and fastened beneath it. Normally it matches the **stole** in colour and decoration. Derived from the Roman *mappar,* it was originally a handkerchief which came to be a rank ornament of the consul, which he used to signal the start of games. It is rarely used today.

MANUAL(E) (Latin, 'book of handy size'). A book containing the forms for the parish priest for administration of sacraments and rites, other than the mass. Known also as the Sacerdotal, it more commonly goes by the name of **ritual.**

MANUAL ACTS. Actions which occur at the communion when the president may take the **paten** into his hands, and/or break the bread and/or lay his hand upon it, and similarly with the chalice. They are often directed by **indented rubrics.**

MATTINS. The traditional **breviary** office for the night (prior to dawn) comprising hymn, psalms, lessons, the Te Deum and collect. It was replaced in the 1971 Breviary by the office of Readings. The structure for Morning Prayer in the BCP is based on Mattins with supplements from **prime,** and the office is often called Mattins.

MEMENTO. (Latin, 'remember'). The initial word of two sections of the Tridentine Roman **canon.** (1)*Memento* of the living *(commemoratio pro vivis)*: in Gallican and Mozarabic rites this precedes **sursum corda,** being associated with the **offertory.** It constitutes the second paragraph of the Roman canon, following **te Igitur;** it was probably included in the fourth century. Originally a list of names of those who had made offerings, it became more general when the faithful no longer gave the bread and wine. (2) *Memento* of the dead *(commemoratio pro defunctis).* Originally used in the West only at funerals and requiems, it later took a regular place in the Roman Canon. Names were formerly recited from the **diptychs,** but came to be read silently.

MISSA CATECHUMENORUM (Latin, 'Mass of the catechumens'). The ante-communion or **synaxis.** It is so named because, owing to the **disciplina arcani,** it was the only part of the eucharist to which catechumens were admitted.

MISSA FIDELIUM (Latin 'Mass of the faithful'). The part of the mass extending from the **offertory** to the end of the service. The name is derived from times when the **disciplina arcani** was practised and the unbaptized catechumens were dismissed so that only the baptized remained to join in the eucharistic offering.

MISSA NORMATIVA. The normative text of the 1970 Roman Mass. Vatican II authorized the translation of the new *Missa Normativa* into the vernacular.

MISSAL(E). The book which brought together the **sacramentary, antiphon** book and the **lectionary.** It evolved between the tenth and thirteenth centuries as a collection of the Mass formularies fostered by the custom of saying private masses. Missals often now omit biblical readings which are issued in a separate Lectionary.

MITRE. Liturgical head dress of a bishop, shield-shaped in the West, originally of white linen but now usually of embroidered satin and sometimes jewelled.

MIXED CHALICE. The mingling of water and wine in the cup at the eucharist. In the early church water and wine were mingled before the elements were brought in, but later the addition of water to wine became a ceremony accompanying the preparation of the elements at the communion table at the time of the **offertory,** and symbolic meanings were attached to it. It is not mentioned in most Anglican rites since 1549, though the practice was revived during the nineteenth century.

MONSTRANCE. A receptacle, often of elaborate design and usually of precious metal, with a central transparent container in which the consecrated **host** is exposed for veneration. Only found in the West.

NARRATIVE OF INSTITUTION. See **Institution Narrative.**

NARTHEX. Common in the Hellenistic styled basilica, the narthex operated as a waiting area before services began. It was utilized anciently for catechumens, the mentally deranged, and penitents. Open to the **nave,** it was the place from which the **great entrance** in its original form began. As a response to the recent changing liturgical movement, several new or rebuilt churches have a form of narthex as a major feature.

NAVE (Latin, *navis* 'ship'). The main body of the church used by the congregation.

NOBIS QUOQUE (Latin, 'to us also'). The final paragraph of the Tridentine Roman **canon,** it is a prayer that we may share in the inheritance of the apostles and martyrs.

NOCTURN. Comparable to the modern **mattins,** although it could be used as a general term applying to the night offices, including **lauds.**

NONE ('ninth'). Last of the 'little hours' which were originally observed at times of private prayer and later were incorporated into the Monastic **office.** None by its name was meant to be said at 3 p.m., although it was often recited immediately following the principal daily Mass at noon. See **prime.**

NORTH SIDE (or **NORTH END**). The practice of the president standing to the north side of the table at the eucharist has evolved from the time of the Reformation when communion tables were placed on an east-west axis in the **nave** or **chancel** of the church and so the president would stand at the north side. As communion tables were replaced in an altar-wise position, the rubric 'The priest standing at the north side of the table . . .' (1662) was interpreted as requiring him to stand still to the north side, thus avoiding the eastward position which had obstructed the congregation's view of the **manual acts.**

O-ANTIPHONS. Also known as the Greater Antiphons, the antiphons which, according to the Roman use, are sung before and after the **magnificat** at **vespers** on the seven days preceding Christmas Eve. The name is derived from their initial 'O', e.g. *'O Sapientia', 'O Adonai', 'O Emmanuel'.* The authorship and date of composition of the O-Antiphons are unknown; but they were already in use by the eighth century.

OBSECRATION. The litany petition beginning with the word 'by' (Latin *'ob'*).

OBLATION. See **Prayer of Oblation.**

OCTAVE. The name given, in Christian liturgical usage, to the period comprising a feast day and the seven days following: thus a total of eight days.

OFFERTORIUM. Chant used at the **offertory.**

OFFERTORY. The name given in the West to the preparation of the eucharistic elements, prior to the **eucharistic prayer.** Cranmer used the name for a collection of money, and both uses are to be found today.

OFFICE (Latin, *officium,* 'duty' or 'service'). The daily public prayers of the church which from the late fifth century included the night office **mattins** and the seven Day Hours—**lauds, prime, terce, sext, none, vespers,** and **compline.** All eight 'hours' consist of psalms, hymns, lessons, antiphons, responses and **versicles** and prayers. The eight offices were replaced in the Church of England by Morning and Evening Prayer (Mattins and Evensong). In 1971, following Vatican II recommendations, a new **breviary** was issued. This provided for an office of Readings to be said anytime during the day (replacing Mattins, Lauds, a mid-day office (see Prime), Vespers, and Compline.)

OFFICIO PRO DEFUNCTIS (Latin 'office for the dead'). Also called **dirge,** it dates from the Middle Ages, normally confined to the Morning Office, but later included **vespers.** In the BCP the dirge is in a modified form containing relevant sentences, psalms, and lesson.

ORDINARY. Those parts of the mass which, unlike the **propers,** do not vary according to the season. It usually refers both to the fixed parts of the **canon** as well as to other features such as **kyrie eleison, gloria in excelsis.**

ORDINES ROMANI. Liturgical books containing instructions for the correct performance of Roman rites, composed in Rome from the seventh to the fifteenth century.

ORNAMENTS RUBRIC. Provision in the BCP, in a note before Morning Prayer, concerning the 'ornaments of the church and ministers'. First inserted in 1552, its 1559 and 1662 forms gave rise to controversy in the nineteenth century.

O SAPIENTIA. The first of the **O Antiphons,** sung on 16 December. It was listed in the 1662 BCP calendar.

PALL. (a) A square white linen cloth to cover the chalice during the ᵉucharist, sometimes stiffened, originally one with the **corporal,** forming a single large cloth on which the chalice and **paten** stood and which could be drawn up over them. (b) A cloth thrown over a free-standing **altar** in order to envelop it on all sides (altar pall/cloth). Also known as a Laudian frontal. (c) A cloth, commonly black, purple, or white, spread over a coffin whilst in church.

PALLIUM. Originally a badge of office worn by Roman consuls and senators, adopted by church dignitaries. A narrow circular band worn over the shoulders, with a strip hanging at the back and front, it was made of white woollen material. It was conferred in the Middle Ages by the Pope on archbishops.

PATEN. A plate or shallow dish on which the bread is placed. Reversed, it may serve as the lid of a chalice.

PEDILAVIUM. The ceremony of 'feet washing' performed during Maundy Thursday liturgy when the president at mass washes and dries the feet of twelve men following the reading of the gospel (John 13). It is also still practised in the Moravian Church, among Seventh Day Adventists, and among some Black Pentecostalists.

PEW. Wooden benches for the congregation, sometimes elaborately carved. Pews were a thirteenth century Western innovation. Previously standing or kneeling was the customary posture, except for the infirm for whom stone ledges were provided around the church walls.

PIE (or **PICA**). The fifteenth century English name for the **ordinale** or **directorium**—the 'book of directions' for saying the services, in relation especially to movable and immovable feasts. Cranmer criticized it, for the number and hardness of its rules, in the Preface to the 1549 BCP ('Concerning the Service of the Church' 1662 BCP).

PISCINA. A stone basin for washing the communion vessels, provided with a drain leading into the ground, generally set in or against the wall to the south side of the **altar.** Originally the latin for fishpond, the connexion is with the early Christian symbol of the fish.

PLACEBO. The service of **vespers** said from mediaeval times for the dead before burial. The name derives from the **antiphon** 'Placebo Domine in regione vivorum' from Ps. 116.9 (see **dirge).**

PLANETA. Alternative name for **chasuble.**

PONTIFICAL(E). A liturgical book for ceremonies and prayers used by a bishop e.g. Confirmation, Ordination, etc.

PORRECTIO INSTRUMENTORIUM (Latin, 'handing over of the instruments'). The ceremony in which the 'tools of the trade' are handed to the newly ordained. Originally confined to candidates for minor orders on whom hands were not laid, it was extended to the other orders in Gallican practice. Cranmer changed the 'instrumenta' from, e.g., chalice and **paten,** to the New Testament or Bible.

PRAYER OF CONSECRATION. See **Consecration, Prayer of.**

PRAYER OF OBLATION. A prayer of self-offering derived from the latter part of the **canon** of 1549, which in 1552 Cranmer detached and turned into an alternative post-communion prayer.

PRECES (Latin, 'prayers'). Responsive prayers in Morning and Evening Prayer in BCP. They are said between the Creed and Collects and may refer specifically to **versicles** in these prayers.

PREFACE (Latin, *praefatio,* 'proclamation'). The first section of the **eucharistic prayer,** after the **sursum corda** in which thanks are given for the work of God in creation and redemption, leading to the **sanctus.** The **proper** preface is the seasonally variable part.

PRESANCTIFIED. The 'Mass of the Presanctified' is celebrated on Good Friday in the Roman Church, using bread and wine consecrated (presanctified) at the previous eucharist. In Eastern Orthodoxy the liturgy of the Presanctified is used on Wednesday and Friday throughout Lent and on the first three days of Holy Week, using elements consecrated on the preceding Sunday.

PRIE-DIEU. Small prayer desk, usually for private use.

PRIME. The first of the 'little hours' appointed to be said at the first hour of the day (i.e. between 6 a.m. and 7 a.m.). Since 1971 the Roman **breviary** requires only one of the 'little hours' to be said as a midday office. See also **terce, sext, none.**

PRIMER. A book of lay devotions popular in early fourteenth century containing the Little Office of B.V.M., some penitential psalms, gradual Psalms, the Litany of the Saints and the Office for the Dead, **dirge.** 1534 saw the first sanctioned English editions, followed by the 'King's Primer' 1545, revised 1552. It was used as an aid in teaching children to read.

PROCESSIONAL(E). Mediaeval service book containing the Litanies, hymns, and prayers, formally prescribed for processions.

PROKEIMENON. The Eastern Orthodox **antiphon,** comprising verses from the Psalter, sung before the epistle in the Byzantine rite. It is probably derived from the saying of a psalm between the, now discarded, Old Testament lesson and the epistle.

PRONE. A vernacular passage in the course of a mass. The prone was a response in the Middle Ages to the virtual disappearance in western liturgy of intercessory prayers and was the continental equivalent to the **bidding of the bedes.**

PROPER (i.e. 'appropriate'). A term referring to those parts of the eucharistic liturgy which vary according to ecclesiastical season, in contrast to the **ordinary** which is fixed through the year. The proper (sometimes 'propers'), include the **introit, gradual** and other chants, together with the readings and proper **preface.**

PROSKOMIDIA. An alternative name for **prothesis,** the preparation of the elements.

PROSPHORA. The sacramental bread of the Eastern Orthodox Churches. Traditionally five loaves are required although the Greek Church now uses only one larger loaf. The bread is solemnly cut up during the **prothesis** and part of each loaf is used for the liturgy; the rest is not consecrated but distributed to the congregation later as the **antidoron.**

PROTHESIS (Greek, 'setting out'). The name of the preparatory office in the Byzantine rite in which the elements are prepared. The word can also be used of the **altar** and of the chamber used for the preparation of the elements.

PULPITUM. A heavy stone screen in a major church provided to shut off the choir from the nave and also to provide a backing for the return choir-stalls. It often contains small chapels or other rooms and may support an organ.

PURIFICATOR. A white linen napkin used to cleanse rim of chalice during administration and to dry the chalice and other vessels during the **ablutions.**

PYX (or **PIX**) (through Latin from Greek, *puxos,* 'box-tree'). Receptacle for housing reserved bread, and sometimes wine. Usually small and suitable for carrying to the sick. Less commonly, a much larger and more elaborate casket suspended by chain (hanging pyx).

QUAM OBLATIONEM (Latin, 'which offering'). The opening words of the fifth paragraph of the Tridentine Roman **canon,** following **hanc igitur.** A prayer requesting that the offering of bread and wine may be consecrated to God and may become for the faithful the Body and Blood of Christ. Its position before the **institution narrative** is that of the **epiclesis** in the early Egyptian **anaphora,** and its role is parallel, though the Holy Spirit is not mentioned.

QUI PRIDIE (Latin, 'who the day before'). The initial words of the first part of the **institution narrative** in the Tridentine Roman **canon,** following **quam oblationem.** See also **simili modo.**

QUIRE (Archaic spelling of 'choir'). See **chancel.**

RED LETTER DAYS. See **black letter days.**

REDDITIO SYMBOLI. The formal recitation of the creed by the baptizands. When the **disciplina arcani** was practised, the catechumens would never previously have heard the Lord's Prayer or creeds. During the preparation, the bishop would teach the **competentes** the creed and its meaning, an occasion known as the *traditio symboli,* or delivery of the creed. They in turn had to repeat it back—the Redditio Symboli—on Holy Saturday before baptism.

REFRESHMENT SUNDAY. The fourth Sunday in Lent, also known as Mothering Sunday.

REREDOS. A framed screen or panelling behind or above an **altar,** usually constructed to fill the gap created between the base of the window and the altar top. A feature of the late Middle Ages, it was often decorated with carved or painted pictures of the saints.

RESPOND. A chant consisting of Scriptural verses to follow a lesson; e.g. **gradual.**

RESPONSARY. A liturgical chant consisting of a series of **versicles** and responses, varying according to the office and season.

RITUAL(E). The official service book for the administration of Baptism, Marriage and a variety of other rites, omitting those services contained in either **breviary** or **missal.** See also **manual.**

ROCHET. A variant form of the **alb,** sleeveless or narrow-sleeved. It was in general clerical use until the thirteenth century, after which it became the prerogative of bishops, cardinals and canons. Originally a functional dust-coat, it became more ornate. It is worn by Anglican bishops under the **chimere.**

ROGATION DAYS (Latin *rogatio,* 'asking'). Days for praying for the crops. Rogation Sunday has popularly been kept on the fifth Sunday after Easter, and the Rogation Days come in the BCP on the Monday, Tuesday and Wednesday following (i.e. before Ascension Day).

ROOD. A crucifix, especially one hanging in the **chancel** or quire entrance. When it is fixed above a screen, it is known as a rood-screen.

SACRAMENTARY. A liturgical book for use by a priest, with all texts needed for celebrating the eucharist, administration of the sacraments, blessings, and rites of ordination. By the thirteenth century each see, church and monastery had its own collection. Gradually replaced by **missal** and **pontificale.**

SANCTORAL(E). Section of **missal** or **breviary** or equivalent containing masses or offices for festivals of particular saints, except those which occur at Christmastide—see **temporal(e).**

SANCTUARY. The space around the **altar** or communion table, usually at the east end of the church. It is usually demarcated by either a rail or a step.

SANCTUS. The anthem 'Holy, Holy, Holy . . .' (drawn from Is. 6.3) usually forming a responsive part of the **eucharistic prayer.**

SCARF. Another name for the **tippett.**

SCRUTINY. The formal examination of the catechumens. In Africa, there was one; in Rome, three. In the modern Roman rite, there are three, held at Mass on the third, fourth and fifth Sundays of the year. Originally the purpose was to ensure that **exorcism** had been successful, that the baptizand was free of unclean spirits. The scrutiny was an elaborate ritual. Later the idea grew that the rite was to ensure that proper instruction had been given, and this holds today in the Roman rite.

SECRET or **SECRETA.** A prayer said or sung by the president after the **offertory** in the Roman tradition at the eucharist. The prayer was originally said silently (hence the name) and it may vary depending upon the **proper** of the day.

SEDILIA. Recessed seats for the assisting priests and deacons (usually three in number), on the south side of the **sanctuary.** Wooden sedilia are not unknown.

SEQUENCE (Latin, *sequentia*). A kind of hymn sung on certain days between the **gradual** and the gospel. *'Dies Irae'* is sung on All Souls' Day.

SEXT. The third of the 'little hours', appointed to be said at midday. See **prime.**

SIMILI MODO (Latin, 'in like manner'). The initial words of the second part of the **institution narrative** in the Tridentine Roman **canon.** The consecratory words over the **chalice,** like those over the **host,** blend scriptural accounts with non-biblical phraseology. (See also **qui pridie).**

SPUTATIO (Latin, 'spitting'). Spitting in the face of Satan during baptismal renunciation.

STATIONAL MASS. In the early church, a celebration of the eucharist at a church, martyr's tomb or other place where ecclesiastical processions made a halt. 'Statio' was the Latin term for Christian assemblies of worship. Until the 1970 revision of Roman rites, days on which the Pope formerly celebrated Mass in 'station-churches' at Rome were marked in the **missal.**

STOLE. A strip of material worn over the shoulders by clergy, deacons wearing it as a sash over the left shoulder, priests and bishops wearing it as a scarf, around the back of the neck, hanging vertically. It usually matches the liturgical colour of the **chasuble** or **dalmatic** and is worn over the **alb** or **surplice,** but under any outer vestments.

SUFFRAGES. Prayers seeking favour and support, penitential or intercessory prayers such as the **litany.** They normally occur in the form of **versicles** and responses, concluding with a collect. An alternative name for **preces.**

SUPPLEMENTARY CONSECRATION. Provision for consecration of further bread and wine when there is insufficient. Various methods are followed.

SUPPLICES TE ROGAMUS. See **supra quae** below.

SUPRA QUAE (Latin, 'upon which'). The initial words of the prayer for acceptance of the eucharistic offering in the Tridentine Roman **canon,** following the **anamnesis (unde et memores)** and preceding the **memento** of the dead. This prayer divides into two paragraphs, embodying rearrangements of ancient liturgical material. The first alludes to Old Testament sacrifices, a feature common to many **anaphoras** but omitted at this point in eucharistic prayers II, III and IV of the revised rite. The second paragraph **(supplices te rogamus)** links the heavenly and the earthly altars. Generally an invocation of the Holy Spirit follows the **anamnesis.** Some liturgists regard **supra quae** as an **epiclesis.**

SURPLICE (Latin, *superpelliceum,* 'over a fur garment'). Wide-sleeved, ample version of the **alb,** adopted in the twelfth century for wear over fur-lined **cassocks** (it goes over the head). Worn by priests for non-eucharistic purposes, and commonly worn today over the cassock by both clergy and lay persons.

SURSUM CORDA (Latin, 'lift up your hearts'). Following the salutation, this call opens the dialogue which begins the **eucharistic prayer.** The response is 'we lift them to the Lord'.

SYNAPTE (Greek, 'joined together'). The great **litany** in the Byzantine rite.

SYNAXIS (Greek, 'gathering together'). Any meeting for public worship but particularly the ministry of the word or ante-communion in the euchar-ist.

TABERNACLE (Latin, 'tent'). A veiled safe or cupboard, standing in a central position at the rear of an **altar** (often a side altar) for the reservation of the sacramental elements.

TE IGITUR (Latin, 'you therefore'). The opening words of the first paragraph of the Tridentine Roman **canon,** possibly inserted here in the fourth century (the significance of *igitur* is uncertain). The prayer asks God to accept and bless the eucharistic offerings, the offerers being named in the next paragraph **memento.**

TEMPORAL(E). Section of **missal, breviary** or equivalent containing variable parts of masses and offices for moveable feasts, which are not provided for in the **sanctorale.**

TENEBRAE (Latin, 'darkness'). The popular name for a combined service of **mattins** or **nocturns** and **lauds.** Provided, from the Middle Ages, for the last three days of Holy Week, but sung by anticipation on the preceding evenings—the *Tenebrae* of Maundy Thursday being sung on Wednesday. The name probably derived from the ceremony of extinguishing, one by one, fourteen out of the fifteen candles set in a triangular stand—symbolizing the apparent victory of the powers of darkness at the crucifixion.

TERCE. The second of the 'little hours', to be said at 9 a.m. (the third hour). See **prime.**

TERSANCTUS (Latin, 'thrice holy'). An alternative name for **trisagion** but sometimes, wrongly, used for the **sanctus.**

THURIBLE (Latin, *tus,* 'incense'). Metal vessel for the ceremonial burning of incense. Usually a container suspended on chains from which it can be swung during the censing. Also known as a censer, it is carried by the **thurifer.**

THURIFER. An assistant or acolyte who carries the **thurible.**

TIPPET. Long black **scarf,** worn by Anglican clergy over the **surplice.**

TRACT. The name given to the chant which was sung or recited at the mass on certain penitential days instead of the **alleluia.** Its position is between the epistle and the gospel. It originally consisted of a psalm.

TRADITIO INSTRUMENTORUM. An alternative name for **porrectio instrumentorum.**

TRANSEPT. The cross arms of a cruciform church projecting out at right-angles to the **nave** and **chancel.**

TRENTAL. A set of thirty masses for the repose of a soul; alternatively a mass said on the thirtieth day after death or burial.

TRIFORIUM. Arcaded wall passage or blank arcading facing the **nave** at the height of the aisle roof and below the **clerestory** windows.

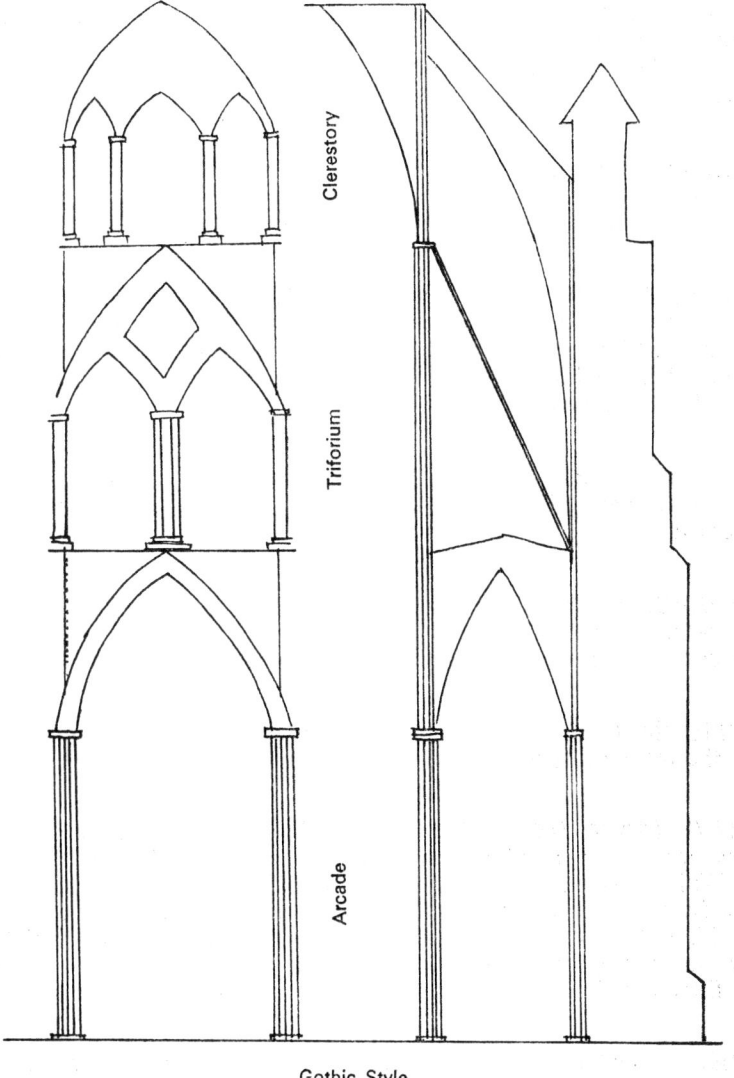

Gothic Style

TRISAGION (Greek, 'thrice holy'). The hymn 'Holy God, Holy and Mighty, Holy and Immortal, Have mercy upon us' is repeated three times after the **little entrance** and at other points in the Byzantine liturgy. (See also **tersanctus**).

TUNICLE. Variant form of the **alb,** similar to the **dalmatic.**

UNCTION. Anointing with holy oil. (See also **extreme unction**).

UNDE ET MEMORES (Latin, 'wherefore also calling to mind'). The opening words and thus title of the **anamnesis** of the Tridentine Roman **canon,** following the **institution narrative (qui pridie** and **simili modo).**

VEIL. Any liturgical cloth used for covering an object, particularly the chalice-veil, which is a cloth (usually of seasonal colour) used to cover the vessels during the **synaxis** and **ablutions**.

VENI CREATOR (Latin, 'Come Creator'). The title of a hymn to the Holy Spirit possibly composed in the ninth century in the Frankish Empire and often attributed to Rabanus Maurus. The best known English version is that of Bishop J. Cosin, 'Come, Holy Ghost, our souls inspire', included in the BCP Ordinal.

VERSICLES. Often taken from psalms, they are single lines of praise or prayer said or sung by the leader of worship, followed by congregational responses.

VESPERS. Together with **lauds,** the oldest of 'day hours' and the most important. The office of Evensong in the BCP was constructed from vespers with additions from **compline**.

VIATICUM (Latin, 'belonging to a journey'). Holy communion given from the reserved sacrament to those in danger of death.

VOTIVE MASS (*Missa Votiva*). A eucharist celebrated by reason of a vow or with a particular intention not in the liturgical calendar for that day. With some exceptions, this may be offered on **feria** outside Lent and Advent and on other days that do not require the Mass of the day to be said. Before Vatican II, Latin **missals** provided a wide variety of votive masses, generally said by choice of the priest. The revised rites have fifteen, which are to serve the devotion of the people.

ZEON. Hot water added to **chalice** at the eucharist in Easter Orthodox churches.